Presented To:

My Ryan "RJ"
Love, mommy
I Love You!

Date:

Dec 21st 2007
Happy Birthday!

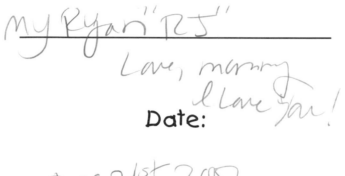

Little Boys Book of Prayers

for Mothers and Sons

Produced by Educational Publishing Concepts, Inc. Wheaton, Illinois.
Published by New Kids Media™ in association with Baker Book House
Company, P.O. Box 6287 Grand Rapids, Michigan 49516-6287.

ISBN 0-8010-4440-5

2 3 4 5 6 7 — 03 02 01 00

Little Boys Book of Prayers

for

Mothers and Sons

Carolyn Larsen
Illustrated by Caron Turk

NEW KiDS MEDIA

Published in
association with

BAKER
A DIVISION OF
Baker Book House Co

Dear Moms,

What a privilege it is to encourage your little boys to make prayer a daily part of their lives. Caron Turk and I hope that The *Little Boys Book of Prayers* will help your little boys learn that they can talk to God about anything and everything.

The prayers in this book are loosely divided into the four forms that prayer takes: Adoration, Confession, Thanksgiving, and Supplication. As you read these prayers with your little boy, I encourage you to personalize them—think of things that your little boy appreciates about God; or things he may need to learn to confess. Help him express to God things that he is thankful for and discuss needs he has or those of people he cares about and bring them before God.

Caron Turk has again created delightful illustrations and has hidden a little boy angel and his lizard buddy in every one. Have fun looking for them!

Caron and I pray that this book will be a blessing to you and your little boy and that it will begin a lifelong habit of daily prayer for your little boy.

Blessings!
Carolyn Larsen

Contents

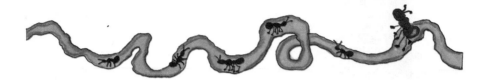

Dear God,

      You sure made some cool bugs! Today I laid on my tummy and watched an ant carry a big crumb. It must have been really strong 'cause the crumb was big and the ant had to work hard to move it. Thank you for making ants.

                    Amen

Dear God,

    It must have been fun to make stuff like big, tall mountains and great big waterfalls and rainbows. They sure are fun to look at. Good job, God.

                        Amen

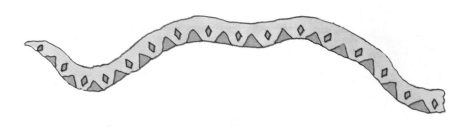

Dear God,

How did you think about letting snakes crawl right out of their skin? I found a snake skin that no snake is using anymore. I like it. That was a good idea.

Amen

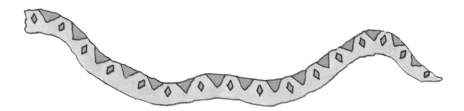

Dear God,
     You must have a lot of love to be able to love everyone in the whole world. That's a lot of people. I guess that's why the Bible says, "God is love." It must be hard to love all the time, thank you for not giving up.

                    Amen

Dear God,

    Sometimes I get tired of forgiving my brother. Momma says you are my example of forgiving 'cause you forgive over and over. I just wondered, do you ever get tired of forgiving people? Momma says you don't—thank you for being so forgiving.

                      Amen

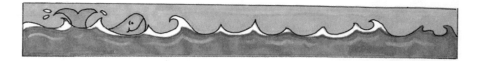

Dear God,

    You made everything there is ... even me! And you take care of everything and all the people in the world. You listen to our prayers and you help us. Thank you for being so smart and for caring about us so much.

                  Amen

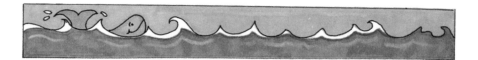

Dear God,
      I can talk to you about
anything. If I'm sad I can tell
you about it. If I'm happy I
know you are happy with me,
too. If I have a problem, you
help me figure it out. Thank you
for caring about me so much.
                                    Amen

Dear Lord,
 You are boss over everything. That must be awesome! Everything does what you say. The sun comes up everyday and the moon and stars shine every night. Rivers flow and animals play in the woods. I'm glad you are the boss cause you know just how everything works best.

 Amen

Dear God,

I just feel like standing on top of something great big and shouting at the top of my lungs, "God is awesome. God is strong! God is love! Everyone should get to know him!" Thank you, God, for being you!

Amen

27

Dear God,

How did you think of making people look so many different ways? Some are short, some are tall, some are skinny and some are round. Some have dark skin and some have white skin. WHEW! You sure had lots of good ideas!

Amen

Dear God,

   Know what I'm glad about? Nothing surprises you. You know when it's going to thunder and lightning, and you know when a big guy is going to pick on me. And, you're always ready for whatever happens!

                    Amen

God knows everything

Dear God,

Mom said that you told the people who wrote all the Bible stories exactly what to write down. She said that's why we say the Bible is God's Word. Wow! You're smart!

Amen

Dear God,

When I watch the news on TV I see a lot of bad things happening everywhere. It makes me nervous that bad things could happen here. I'm glad you have everything under control. You can take care of everything.

Amen

Dear Lord,
    Wow! There must be a
zillion stars in the sky. How
many did you make anyway?
What makes them stay where
you put them? I like how they
twinkle like Christmas lights.
They cheer up the dark night.
                        Amen

Dear God,

   I just saw a chameleon.
You made it so it can change
it's skin color to match
wherever it is. That way it can
hide from it's enemies. What a
great idea!

                    Amen

Dear Father,

I like the story about Joshua and his army marching around Jericho until the walls fell down. You think of the neatest ways to help your people!

Amen

But for six days the Israelites just silently marched around the city— once a day.

...and the walls came tumbling down!

JERICHO

Dear God,
    I feel bad 'cause I cheated when I was playing a game with my friend—just 'cause I wanted to win. After I won I didn't even feel good because I knew that I didn't win fair. I'm sorry I cheated. Please forgive me, and help my friend to forgive me, too.

Amen

Dear God,
My little brother makes me so mad! He always wants to be with me and my friends and he follows us everywhere. Sometimes we run really fast to get away from him. I feel bad when we do that. I'm sorry I'm mean to him, please forgive me and help me to be nicer.

Amen

Dear God,

    I threw a ball in the house, which I'm not supposed to do, and a vase got broken. When Mom asked me about it I lied and said I didn't do it. Now, Mom thinks the dog did it and she made him go outside. I'm sorry I lied. Please help me tell Mom the truth.

                      Amen

Dear God,

I got so mad at my friend today. I threw a toy at him and knocked down the town we built with blocks. I don't feel very good when I do things like that. I'm sorry I lost my temper. Please forgive me and God, please help my friend to give me another chance.

Amen

Dear Father,

I feel crummy. I promised Mom I would clean out my newt's cage—but I didn't. Mom said it will be hard for her to trust my promises if I don't keep them. I'm sorry I broke my promise. I asked Mom to forgive me, will you please forgive me, too?

Amen

Dear Lord,

    I took a yo-yo from a store without paying for it. No one knows, except you and me. I'm scared to tell Mom. She'll probably say I have to take it to the store and tell them what I did. Will you please forgive me, and help me tell Mom?

Amen

Dear Father,

I hope you didn't hear what I said today. Mom calls those words "swears." I heard some kids at school say them and when I got mad they just popped out. I'm really sorry, help me to talk in a way that makes you proud of me.

Amen

Dear Father,
      Someone is always telling me what to do. I get tired of obeying, so sometimes I just don't. Could you help me be better at obeying? Help me remember that people usually want me to obey for my own good.

                                                Amen

Dear God,

   I keep making the same mistakes over and over. I don't mean to, but I do. You are so patient and you forgive me every time I ask you to. Thank you that you love me no matter what! I'm really glad you do.

                                Amen

Dear God,

I'm sorry to tell you this but sometimes I don't like church. That's 'cause sometimes it's boring and they use grown-up words and I have to sit still for so long! I was wondering, would you just help me pay better attention so I can learn more about you?

Amen

Dear God,

The Bible says that you love me no matter what. Sometimes I'm not so easy to love. That's cause sometimes I don't obey and sometimes I say things that aren't very nice. Thank you for loving me even when I'm not being very nice.

Amen

Dear God,

The ocean is about the most awesome thing I ever saw. I like how the waves race in to the shore, then back away and race in again. Thank you for the ocean.

Amen

Dear God,

Do you like it when you hear a baby laughing? I do. It makes me feel happy inside and pretty soon I'm laughing, too. Thank you for making babies and laughter and happy things.

Amen

Ha Ha Ha Ha

Dear God,

    You must like colorful things. You made green grass and blue sky and a yellow sun and a million colors of flowers. Happy colors make me feel good. Thank you for happy colors.

                  Amen

Dear God,
    One of your ideas I like is the way leaves change colors in the fall. I just wish they would stay on the trees longer before they fall off. I think it would be nice if some of them stayed orange and red all year, don't you?

                        Amen

Dear God,

Thank you for loving me when I'm sleeping. Thank you for loving me when I'm playing. Thank you for loving me when I'm helping my mom make cookies. Thank you for loving me all the time. I love you, too.

Amen

Dear God,

My mom is the just-exactly-right-for-me mom. She is good at playing baseball and she makes good sandwiches. She makes me laugh and she snuggles on the couch and reads to me. You did a good job choosing my mom.

Amen

Dear God,

    My dad is awesome. He knows all about cars and he teaches me lots of stuff like how to paint and how to hit a golf ball. Also, my dad makes the best pancakes in the the whole world. But the best thing about my dad is how much he loves me! Thanks for my dad.

                               Amen

My Dad ♥ is awesome.........

Yeah Dad!

Dad is the Best!

I ♥ Love my dad

BLESS OUR HOME

CARS

DEAR GOD Thank You for my dad.

DAD

Dear God,

Mom and Dad work hard to take care of our family. They work at their jobs and then they do stuff at home like laundry, and cleaning, and cutting the grass. They do stuff with me, too, like playing a game or reading a book. I love my mom and dad. Thank you for putting us in the same family.

Amen

Dear Father,
    At first I didn't like my baby sister much 'cause she took lots of Mom's time. When I wanted Mom to play or read to me she was busy doing stuff for the baby. Then one day my sister smiled at me and held onto my finger real tight. Now I think I like being a big brother. Thank you for my sister.

                    Amen

Dear God,

    Thank you for my dog. She runs and plays with me. She's really strong when we play tug-of-war with her chew bone. She knows when I need to be quiet and think. That's when she just lays down beside me and stays still. She's a great pet.

                    Amen

Dear God,

   Thank you for Bible stories.
My favorite is the one when
David beat Goliath. David was
just a little guy and he beat the
big giant that all the soldiers
were scared of. Thank you that
little guys can win when you
help them.

                    Amen

Dear Father,

School is fun! Well, some days I don't want to go and some days it's hard. But I'm glad I can learn new things. My teacher makes the lessons interesting and it's fun to be with my friends. So, thank you for my school.

Amen

Dear God,

I love my grandma and grandpa! They tell me funny stories about when Mom was a little girl. Grandma makes good cookies and Grandpa teaches me fun stuff like fishing. Thank you for my grandma and grandpa, they are the best!

Amen

Dear Father,

Yahoo! It's my birthday! We're going to have a big party with cake and ice cream and games and PRESENTS and all my friends are coming. Thank you for birthdays and for friends and family to celebrate with!

Amen

Dear God,

My momma says I'm really good at making a joyful noise! I can sing really loud! Thank you for music and singing and drums and guitars and all kinds of ways to make music.

Amen

a joyful noise

Dear God,

Snow is awesome! I like to sled really fast down big hills and I like to make snow angels. You thought of a good kind of snow that packs together to make snowballs and I can make a snowman or build a snowfort and play with my friends. Thank you for snow!

Amen

Dear God,
 Thank you for making food. It was a good idea to make healthy food green or orange. That way I know when I'm getting "this-is-good-for-you" food. (Most of it's OK, but I wish you would have skipped green beans.)
                    Amen

Dear God,

Yahoo! We're going on vacation. Our whole family is going to stay in a tent and we'll cook dinner at the campfire and make s'mores. We can swim in the lake and go fishing and hiking. (I hope we see a bear!) It's going to be so fun! Thank you for vacation time!

Amen

Dear God,
     Know what I like?
Airplanes. Old fashioned ones
with double wings and fancy
new ones like the Stealth.
Thank you for helping someone
think of how to build neat things
like airplanes.

                Amen

Dear God,
    I'm really glad we have doctors. My arm broke when I fell off my bike and it really hurt. The doctor made it feel better and he put an awesome red cast on it. Thank you for my doctor who knows how to take care of me.

                                    Amen

Dear God,
   Did you know how much fun mud puddles would be? It's fun to jump and splash and get mud in my ears and hair and everywhere. It feels gross to squish mud between my toes ... I like it! Thank you for thinking of mud.

                              Amen

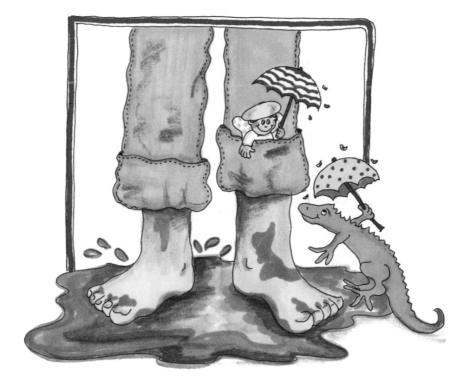

Dear God,

I'm glad I can't play hide and seek from you. No matter where I go or what I do . . . you know where I am. And, you take care of me, no matter what! Thanks for always being there!

Amen

Dear Father,

My favorite holiday is Thanksgiving. Mom starts cooking turkey early in the morning and it smells so good that my mouth waters all day. A bunch of people come to eat with us and we have pumpkin pie and ice cream for dessert. Thank you for Thanksgiving!

Amen

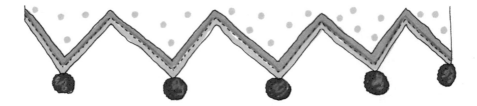

Dear God,

You must love us a lot to send your Son to live on earth. Were you sad when Jesus left heaven? Thank you for sending him. That's the best Christmas present ever!

Amen

Dear God,

Know what is the best thing about Christmas? Presents! But, not my presents—I like when we do a Giving Tree and give presents to kids that might not get any otherwise. We give them in secret, too, so no one knows we gave them, except us . . . and you!

Amen

Dear God,

    You must have been really sad when Jesus was arrested and then people killed him. He only came to earth to tell us that you love us. I'm sorry that had to happen.

                  Amen

Dear God,

Was there shouting and cheering in heaven on that first Easter morning when Jesus came back to life? Thank you for coming up with such a great plan so we can be in heaven with you forever.

Amen

Dear God,

Wow! Did you see how fast I can run and how high I can jump? Thank you that I'm getting bigger and stronger. Thank you that I'm growing up!

Amen

Dear God,
       Know what I like best
about summer? Swimming!
Yeah, I like splashing and
jumping and diving for pennies
with my friends. Thank you for
hot summer days and for
swimming pools!
                          Amen

Dear God,
    Why does Mom get so upset about dirt anyway? It's fun to play in the dirt with my cars and make roads and hills. Sometimes my friends and I make mud and have mud fights. Mom doesn't like that much. Thanks for dirt and mud.
                        Amen

Dear God,

I like hearing stories from the Bible; especially the ones about big battles with lots of swords and spears and chariots. Thanks for putting such cool stories in the Bible, they're fun to read about.

Amen

BIBLE ★ STORIES

...and God showed
how much he loved
us with a Rainbow...

Dear Lord,

    I'm glad I have friends. If I didn't, I would throw a ball and no one would throw it back. Or, when I go hide, no one would look for me. Thanks for thinking of friends. They make life more fun!

                          Amen

Dear God,
  Thank you that my mom and dad take me to church and they read Bible stories to me and they say prayers with me every night. I'm glad they love you and that they teach me how to know you better.
                                    Amen

Dear Father,

Wow! I thought winter would never end! Snow is fun and winter stuff is OK, except it lasts way too long! Today I saw some flowers peeking up through the dirt and buds coming on the trees. Yahoo! Spring is here!

Amen

Dear Father,
   Thank you for
thunderstorms. Mom and I sit
by the window and watch the
lightning bolts race through the
clouds. When the thunder gets
really noisy we shout as loud as
we can. You're really powerful
and strong. I'm glad we're on
the same side!

                    Amen

Dear Lord,
    Thank you for my country.
Thank you that we're free here
and we can go to any church
we want and we can tell
people about you. Thank you
that we have food and that
there isn't a war going on here.
Thank you for my country.
                        Amen

Dear God,

Thank you that I can talk to you about anything I want, anytime I want. Thank you for caring about everything that is important to me. I love you, God.

Amen

Dear God,

I need some help here. My mom says I need to learn self-control 'cause when I eat one cookie, then I want to eat six cookies. Please help me learn to really enjoy one cookie and not want five more, even if they are chocolate chip.

Amen

Dear Father,

My friend hurt my feelings 'cause he said mean things to me. I said that I didn't want to be his friend anymore until I remembered that you always forgive me when I do wrong things. I guess I should forgive my friend, too. But, I'm going to need your help.

Amen

Dear God,

I know you are supposed to be the most important thing to me. I do love you, but I love other people, too, like my mom and dad. I know that it's OK that I love them, but what if I love them more than I love you? Please help me learn how to make you the most important thing in my life.

Amen

Dear God,

    I saw a story on TV about some people who don't have homes. I feel sad for them 'cause they don't have anyplace to go when it's cold and rainy outside. They don't have a place to keep stuff or a place that is just their own. Take care of those people God, keep them safe.

                    Amen

Dear God,

    How come people have to get old anyway? My grandpa used to play catch with me and take me fishing and do all kinds of fun stuff. But he doesn't do anything anymore. I miss the way Grandpa used to be.

Amen

Dear God,

Don't tell anyone this, OK? I'm scared. My daddy is really sick. I guess I'm afraid he might die. I know that you can make sick people well, so would you please help my dad get better?

Amen

Dear God,

My best friend is moving away. I'll miss him cause we like to do the same things and we have so much fun together. He's kind of nervous about moving to a new town. Will you help him find new friends? And, please don't let him forget me!

Amen

Dear God,

How come people that used to love each other stop loving each other? My mom and dad are getting a divorce and our house isn't very happy right now. It's hard cause it seems like everywhere I go I see moms and dads and kids doing stuff together. I miss us being us.

Amen

Dear God,

Sometimes at night when my room is dark, I get a little scared. I see all kinds of ugly, scary things in the shadows. I don't like that I can't see what's going on in my room when it's dark. Help me remember that you're with me, even in the dark—especially in the dark!

Amen

Dear God,

The Golden Rule says, "Do unto others as you would have them do unto you." Right now I want to punch my friend in the nose ... but I don't want him to punch me back. Please help me be kind, even when he is being mean.

Amen

Dear God,

I've never been in the hospital before, except when I was being born and I don't remember that. Mom says I'm just going to have a simple operation and I'll be home the next day. So, help me be brave and help the doctor to not make any mistakes.

Amen

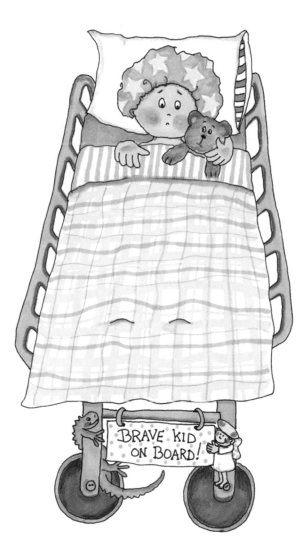

Dear God,

My dad lost his job. What if he can't find another job? Will we have to move out of our house? Where will we get food? God, please help him find another job right away. And, take care of us until he does.

Amen

Dear God,

I make me so mad! I try so hard not to fight with my brother, but I end up beating him up anyway. I'm really sorry. Will you please help me to stop the fighting? Thanks.

Amen

Dear God,

    I don't like my teacher so much. Sometimes it seems like she's mean and it feels like she is picking on me. Will you please help me to be respectful and polite to her. Help me to not do the things that make her upset.

Amen

Dear God,

  We are moving to a new town cause Dad got transferred. I don't want to go! I'll miss my friends and my soccer team. What if I can't make the team in my new town? Help me, God, cause I'm scared.

                              Amen

Dear God,

My head hurts and my tummy is rolling all around. I guess I'm sick. I don't like to be sick, but I'm really glad for my mom. She takes good care of me when I don't feel good. Please help me to get better soon.

                                        Amen

Dear Father,

Will you please help my friend? He has a hard time in school and some other kids make fun of him. I think he's a really nice guy, so please help me to stand up for him. Help the other guys to be nicer to him. Thank you.

Amen

Dear God,

    Why do kids have to get sick? My friend has leukemia. The medicine made all his hair fall out and he is really sick. He might even die. God, I know stories in the Bible when you made sick people well. Please, help my friend get better.

                Amen

Dear God,

My soccer team has it's first game tomorrow. Every time I think about it my heart starts beating really fast and my hands get sweaty. Please help me to not be nervous. Help me play good.

Amen

Dear God,

My friend doesn't go to Sunday school or church. I don't think he believes you are real. I want to invite him to go with me, but I'm kind of scared. Help me be brave enough to ask him. I want him to know you.

Amen

Dear Lord,

I'm really sad today because my dog died. She was pretty old, but she always slept in my room and she was a good soccer player—chasing the ball when I kicked it to her. I'm going to miss her a lot. Thanks for listening.

Amen

Dear Father,

I have to play in my first piano recital tonight. I'm kind of nervous. I know my piece and at home I can play it really good. But, I'm afraid that my hands will get sweaty and start shaking and I'll make lots of mistakes. Help me to not be nervous. Thanks.

Amen

Dear God,
    I got a bad grade on a test today. I try so hard and I study lots, but sometimes the stuff doesn't stick in my brain. I feel dumb, but I KNOW I'M NOT!! Help me to do better next time.

Amen

Dear God,

If you want me to be friends with you-know-who, you're going to have to help me. All she wants to play is house and dolls. Yuck. Please help me be nice 'cause I think I'm out of patience.

Amen

Dear God,

　　When I see on the news about people in other countries where there are wars all the time, I feel bad for them. Why do people have to fight anyway? Help them stop fighting. Help them to take time-outs and settle their problems without shooting at each other.

　　　　　　　　Amen

Dear God,

How come when people get old they can't hear too good or see very well? Sometimes they have trouble walking, too. Do their parts wear out? Help me take good care of myself so my parts last a long time.

Amen